THE HUMAN BEHIND
TOM HOLLAND
IS SPIDER-MAN®

HOT TOPICS

BY KATIE KAWA

Gareth Stevens
PUBLISHING

Please visit our website, www.garethstevens.com. For a free color catalog of all our high-quality books, call toll free 1-800-542-2595 or fax 1-877-542-2596.

Cataloging-in-Publication Data

Names: Kawa, Katie.
Title: Tom Holland is Spider-Man ® / Katie Kawa.
Description: New York : Gareth Stevens Publishing, 2020. | Series: The human behind the hero | Includes a glossary and index.
Identifiers: ISBN 9781538248393 (pbk.) | ISBN 9781538248416 (library bound) | ISBN 9781538248409 (6 pack)
Subjects: LCSH: Holland, Tom,– 1996—Juvenile literature. | Motion picture actors and actresses–Great Britain–Biography–Juvenile literature.
Classification: LCC PN2598.T655 K39 2020 | DDC 791.4302'8092 B–dc23

First Edition

Published in 2020 by
Gareth Stevens Publishing
111 East 14th Street, Suite 349
New York, NY 10003

Designer: Sarah Liddell
Editor: Katie Kawa

Photo credits: Cover, pp. 1, 5 Tinseltown/Shutterstock.com; halftone texture used throughout gn8/Shutterstock.com; comic frame used throughout KID_A/Shutterstock.com; p. 7 Ian West - PA Images/Contributor/PA Images/Getty Images; p. 9 Kevork Djansezian/Stringer/Getty Images Entertainment/Getty Images; p. 11 Jeff Vespa/Contributor/WireImage/Getty Images; pp. 13, 23 Chung Sung-Jun/Staff/Getty Images Entertainment/Getty Images; p. 15 Todd Williamson/Contributor/Getty Images Entertainment/Getty Images; p. 17 Jaguar PS/Shutterstock.com; p. 19 Bobby Bank/Contributor/GC Images/Getty Images; p. 21 DFree/Shutterstock.com; p. 25 Josiah Kamau/Contributor/BuzzFoto/Getty Images; p. 27 Matt Winkelmeyer/Staff/Getty Images Entertainment/Getty Images; p. 29 Victor Chavez/Contributor/WireImage/Getty Images.

Printed in the United States of America

Some of the images in this book illustrate individuals who are models. The depictions do not imply actual situations or events.

CPSIA compliance information: Batch #CW20GS: For further information contact Gareth Stevens, New York, New York at 1-800-542-2595.

CONTENTS

THE FIRST MCU SPIDER-MAN

Tom Holland isn't the first actor to play Spider-Man in a movie. However, he's the first actor to play him in the **Marvel Cinematic Universe** (MCU). Tom is young and talented, and he loves playing a superhero. That's made him a **popular** Spider-Man!

BEHIND THE SCENES

SPIDER-MAN, WHO'S ALSO KNOWN AS PETER PARKER, WAS PLAYED BY TOBEY MAGUIRE IN THREE MOVIES FROM 2002 TO 2007. THEN, ANDREW GARFIELD PLAYED THE PART IN 2012 AND 2014.

EARLY LIFE IN ENGLAND

Tom plays a popular American superhero, but he isn't from the United States. He was born in England on June 1, 1996, and his full name is Thomas Stanley Holland. Tom comes from a close family and has three younger brothers.

BEHIND THE SCENES

TOM LOVES DOGS. HIS DOG TESSA IS AN IMPORTANT PART OF HIS LIFE. TOM SOMETIMES CALLS HER TESS, AND HE LIKES TO SHARE PICTURES AND VIDEOS OF HER.

DANCING THROUGH LIFE

Tom is a talented dancer! He took dance classes while he was growing up. He's also good at doing flips and other kinds of tricks. This training is one of the reasons why he was chosen to be Spider-Man.

BEHIND THE SCENES

TOM WAS IN A **MUSICAL** CALLED *BILLY ELLIOT* IN ENGLAND FROM 2008 TO 2010. AT FIRST, HE PLAYED A CHARACTER NAMED MICHAEL. THEN, HE PLAYED BILLY, WHO'S THE STAR OF THE SHOW!

A SUCCESSFUL START

Tom's first big part in a movie came in 2012 when he played Lucas in *The Impossible*. Many people thought Tom was one of the best parts of the movie, which told the story of a family trying to find each other after a **tsunami**.

IBLE

BEHIND THE SCENES

TOM ACTED IN OTHER MOVIES AFTER THE IMPOSSIBLE, INCLUDING *IN THE HEART OF THE SEA* IN 2015. CHRIS HEMSWORTH, WHO PLAYS THOR IN THE MCU, WAS ALSO IN THAT MOVIE.

11

THE PATH TO PETER PARKER

The next part Tom wanted to play was Peter Parker, but he had to try out for it first. Thousands of actors tried out for the part, but Tom was finally chosen in 2015. He found out he got the part online!

BEHIND THE SCENES

TOM HAD TO DO PRACTICE SCENES
WITH DIFFERENT MCU STARS BEFORE
HE BECAME SPIDER-MAN. WHEN HE DID
A SCENE WITH CHRIS EVANS, WHO PLAYED
CAPTAIN AMERICA, HE SURPRISED
EVERYONE BY DOING A FLIP!

SPIDER-MAN AND IRON MAN

One of the biggest reasons why Tom got the part of Spider-Man was because he acted well with Robert Downey Jr., who played Iron Man. Iron Man and Spider-Man had many important scenes together in the MCU.

ROBERT DOWNEY JR.

BEHIND THE SCENES

TOM AND ROBERT WORKED TOGETHER OUTSIDE OF THE MCU TOO. TOM'S VOICE WAS USED IN THE MOVIE *THE VOYAGE OF DOCTOR DOLITTLE*, WHICH STARS ROBERT AS DOCTOR DOLITTLE.

CHOOSING SIDES

Tom's first movie in the MCU was *Captain America: Civil War*, which came out in 2016. In this movie, many different Marvel heroes fight each other, including Captain America and Iron Man. Spider-Man is on Iron Man's side in the movie's big fight scene.

BEHIND THE SCENES

TOM IS BRITISH, BUT HE HAS TO TALK LIKE AN AMERICAN WHEN PLAYING PETER PARKER. HE'S SAID HE PRACTICES HIS AMERICAN ACCENT, OR WAY OF SPEAKING, IN THE SHOWER!

HIS OWN MOVIE

Fans enjoyed Tom's work in *Captain America: Civil War,* and they wanted to see him star in his own Spider-Man movie. Their wish was granted in 2017. That year, *Spider-Man: Homecoming* opened. Many people said Tom was their **favorite** Spider-Man!

BEHIND THE SCENES

TOM PRETENDED TO BE A HIGH SCHOOL **STUDENT** AT A SCHOOL IN NEW YORK CITY TO PREPARE TO PLAY PETER PARKER. HE USED A FAKE NAME SO NO ONE WOULD KNOW WHO HE WAS.

19

A MEMORABLE MCU MOMENT

In 2018, Tom joined many MCU actors in *Avengers: Infinity War*. Parts of the movie were very sad, but that didn't stop it from being a popular movie. Tom acted in one of the movie's saddest and most **memorable** scenes with Robert Downey Jr.

INFINITI®
POWER THE DRIVE™

AVENGERS
INFINITY WAR

MARVEL STUDIOS
VENGERS
INFINITY WAR

COMICAVE
STUDIOS

COMICAV
STUDIOS

STUDIOS
GERS
WAR

MARVEL STU

BEHIND THE SCENES

IN *INFINITY WAR*, WHEN SPIDER-MAN IS BEING TURNED TO DUST, HE TELLS IRON MAN THAT HE DOESN'T WANT TO GO. TOM CAME UP WITH THAT ON HIS OWN—WITH SOME HELP FROM ROBERT DOWNEY JR.

PART OF THE ENDGAME

Fans wanted answers after

Infinity War, and they got them

the next year when *Avengers:*

Endgame opened. Tom played

Spider-Man again in this movie.

He also got to share more

memorable scenes with Robert.

Endgame became one of the most

successful superhero movies ever!

BEHIND THE SCENES

AVENGERS: ENDGAME MADE MORE THAN $1.2 BILLION AROUND THE WORLD IN ITS OPENING WEEKEND. THAT'S A WORLD RECORD! IN TOTAL, IT MADE MORE THAN $2 BILLION.

23

FAR FROM HOME

Endgame opened in 2019, and that same year, Tom also starred in *Spider-Man: Far From Home*. Jake Gyllenhaal was also in this movie as Mysterio, who's a well-known character from Spider-Man comic books. *Spider-Man: Far From* Home was another success for the MCU!

ZENDAYA

BEHIND THE SCENES

TOM IS CLOSE WITH ZENDAYA, WHO PLAYED MICHELLE JONES—ALSO KNOWN AS M.J.—IN *SPIDER-MAN: HOMECOMING* AND *SPIDER-MAN: FAR FROM HOME*. SHE'S AN ACTRESS, SINGER, DANCER, AND WRITER.

WHAT'S NEXT?

Tom acts in other movies outside of the MCU, and his voice is sometimes used in movies too. For example, his voice is used in the movie *Onward*. This movie also uses the voice of Chris Pratt, who plays Star-Lord in the MCU.

BEHIND THE SCENES

TOM LIKES MAKING PEOPLE
HAPPY AND HELPING THOSE IN NEED.
HE SOMETIMES VISITS KIDS WHO
ARE SICK WHILE WEARING HIS
SPIDER-MAN SUIT!

A POPULAR HERO

Spider-Man first appeared in comic books in 1962. More than 50 years later, he's still one of the most popular superheroes. By bringing this hero to life, Tom Holland has become one of the most well-known young actors in the world!

BEHIND THE SCENES

TOM IS OFTEN ON **SOCIAL MEDIA.**
HE SHARES PICTURES AND VIDEOS OF
HIMSELF WITH HIS FAMILY AND FRIENDS,
AND HE USES SOCIAL MEDIA TO SHARE
NEWS ABOUT HIS MOVIES.

TIMELINE

1996 TOM HOLLAND IS BORN IN ENGLAND ON JUNE 1.

2008 TOM BEGINS HIS TIME IN THE MUSICAL *BILLY ELLIOT*.

2010 TOM ENDS HIS TIME IN *BILLY ELLIOT*.

2012 TOM PLAYS THE PART OF LUCAS IN *THE IMPOSSIBLE*.

2015 TOM IS CHOSEN TO PLAY SPIDER-MAN.

2016 SPIDER-MAN APPEARS IN THE MCU FOR THE FIRST TIME IN *CAPTAIN AMERICA: CIVIL WAR*.

2017 *SPIDER-MAN: HOMECOMING* OPENS.

2018 *AVENGERS: INFINITY WAR* OPENS.

2019 TOM PLAYS SPIDER-MAN IN *AVENGERS: ENDGAME* AND *SPIDER-MAN: FAR FROM HOME*.

FOR MORE INFORMATION

BOOKS

Grange, Emma. *The Amazing Book of Spider-Man*. New York, NY: DK Publishing, 2017.

Hansen, Grace. *Stan Lee: Comic Book Writer & Creator of Spider-Man*. Minneapolis, MN: Abdo Kids, 2018.

Orr, Nicole. *Tom Holland*. Kennett Square, PA: Purple Toad Publishing, 2018.

WEBSITES

IMDb: Tom Holland
www.imdb.com/name/nm4043618/
Tom Holland's Internet Movie Database page has facts about his life and his movies.

Marvel HQ: Games
www.marvelhq.com/games
The Marvel HQ website has many games Marvel fans can play that deal with their favorite superheroes, including Spider-Man.

Marvel: Spider-Man
www.marvel.com/characters/spider-man-peter-parker
The official Marvel website gives fans a closer look at Peter Parker's story.

Publisher's note to educators and parents: Our editors have carefully reviewed these websites to ensure that they are suitable for students. Many websites change frequently, however, and we cannot guarantee that a site's future contents will continue to meet our high standards of quality and educational value. Be advised that students should be closely supervised whenever they access the internet.

31

GLOSSARY

favorite: liked best

Marvel Cinematic Universe: the group of Marvel movies and TV shows that share many of the same characters and began with *Iron Man* in 2008

memorable: not easily forgotten

musical: a play that uses singing, music, and dancing to tell a story

popular: liked by many people

social media: websites and applications, also known as apps, used to create online communities

student: someone who goes to a school to learn

tsunami: a huge wave of water created by an underwater earthquake or volcano

INDEX